Puffin Books

Grimblegraw and the Wuthering Witch

'Bother princesses!' said Prince Benedict, and he changed out of his tunic of scarlet velvet into a plain green one, and ran away.

'Boys!' said Princess Yolanda. 'I've come all this way, in a jolting coach, just to be married to one!' and then *she* took off her glittering dress for one of plain linen, and tiptoed out of the palace.

Later that day they met one another, just by accident (though neither of them had any idea who the other one was!) and as they were both runaways and both wanted adventures, they went along together to look for some. Their first adventure arrived soon enough, in the shape of the terrible Giant Grimblegraw, who grabbed them both and took them home to his castle to cook and clean for him. There they would remain for ever in the Giant's kitchen unless they could outwit the wicked Wuthering Witch and reverse the spell that had made the giant so horrible. But there were two large snags to that plan: firstly, the Giant kept them trapped on a very high shelf, and secondly, as soon as they set eyes on the witch they would be turned to stone!

This lively modern fairy story by the author of *Carbonel* and *Ninety-nine Dragons*, is richly decorated with illustrations by Glenys Ambrus, to make it a volume to remember and cherish.

Grimblegraw and the Wuthering Witch

Barbara Sleigh

Pictures by Glenys Ambrus

PUFFIN BOOKS

Puffin Books,
Penguin Books Ltd, Harmondsworth,
Middlesex, England
Penguin Books, 625 Madison Avenue,
New York, New York 10022, U.S.A.
Penguin Books Australia Ltd, Ringwood,
Victoria, Australia
Penguin Books Canada Ltd, 2801 John Street,
Markham, Ontario, Canada L3R 1B4
Penguin Books (N.Z.) Ltd, 182–190 Wairau Road,
Auckland 10, New Zealand

First published by Hodder & Stoughton Children's Books 1978
Published in this extended edition by Puffin Books 1979

Made and printed in Great Britain by
Richard Clay (The Chaucer Press) Ltd, Bungay, Suffolk
Set in Monotype Baskerville

'Girls!' said Prince Benedict scornfully. 'Simpering, giggling, feather-brained creatures; especially princesses. And now I've got to marry one I've never seen!'

'Dear me,' said the Gentleman of the Bed-Chamber. 'I am sure that does not describe the charming young princess who even now may be waiting to meet you. If I could suggest that the royal right leg might be raised a little higher, so that I can put on the other silk stocking?'

'Oh, bother the other silk stocking!' grumbled the Prince. 'And bother princesses, all the lot of them!' And he jumped to his feet and ran from the room.

Once in the closet next door, he changed his scarlet velvet tunic for one of sober green, slung his legs over the window-sill, and climbed down the ivy that grew outside, with an ease that suggested it was not for the first time.

'Boys!' said Princess Yolanda, in another palace, not far away. 'Boring, bossy, boastful creatures. And I've come all this way, in a jolting coach, just to be married to one!'

'For shame!' said her old nurse. 'Such a handsome young man as they say he is! Now take that sulky look off your face, and let me put on your silver slippers. He will be waiting so eagerly to meet you!'

'Then he can go on waiting!' said the Princess. 'Anyway, the silver slippers pinch!' And she kicked them off and ran from the room. Then she wriggled out of her glittering gown, and put on one of plain blue linen. This done, she tiptoed down the back-stairs.

No one saw her slip quietly out of a side door of the palace.

Prince Benedict whistled cheerfully as he marched along the road away from the town. 'This walking is thirsty work!' he said presently. And hearing the sound of running water, he turned off the road.

The stream was not far away, and sitting on the bank beside it was a girl in a blue linen dress. She was bathing one of her feet.

'Have you hurt it?' he asked.

She nodded. 'It's a blister, I think. I came away – well, in rather a hurry, and I forgot to put on sensible shoes.'

'Let me bandage it for you,' said Benedict. 'Where are you going?'

'I've no idea!' said the girl airily. 'As a matter of fact, I'm running away!'

Benedict sat back on his heels and laughed. 'I'm running away too!' he said. And then they both laughed. 'I've made up my mind to go out into the world and find adventures.'

'That's just what I thought of doing!' said the girl.

'But girls don't do that sort of thing!' said Benedict.

'Why shouldn't they?' she asked.

'All right,' said Benedict, 'let's go on and have adventures together.

What's your name? Mine is – er – er – John.'

'And mine is – is – Jane,' said the girl. And off they went, side by side.

Towards evening, she said suddenly: 'When we started out this morning, all the carts and carriages were going this way and that. Why are they all racing back to the town now? And why is everyone looking behind them

in a frightened sort of way, whipping up their horses and running as fast as they can? Even that old man on crutches is trying to hurry!'

'Good gracious, I'd quite forgotten!' said John. 'It's because of Giant Grimblegraw.'

'Whoever is Giant Grimblegraw?' asked Janc.

'Have you never heard of him?' said John. 'He is a terrible fellow! As tall as the Town Hall, they say. Each foot is as big as a bath and his eyes whizz round like Catherine-wheels.

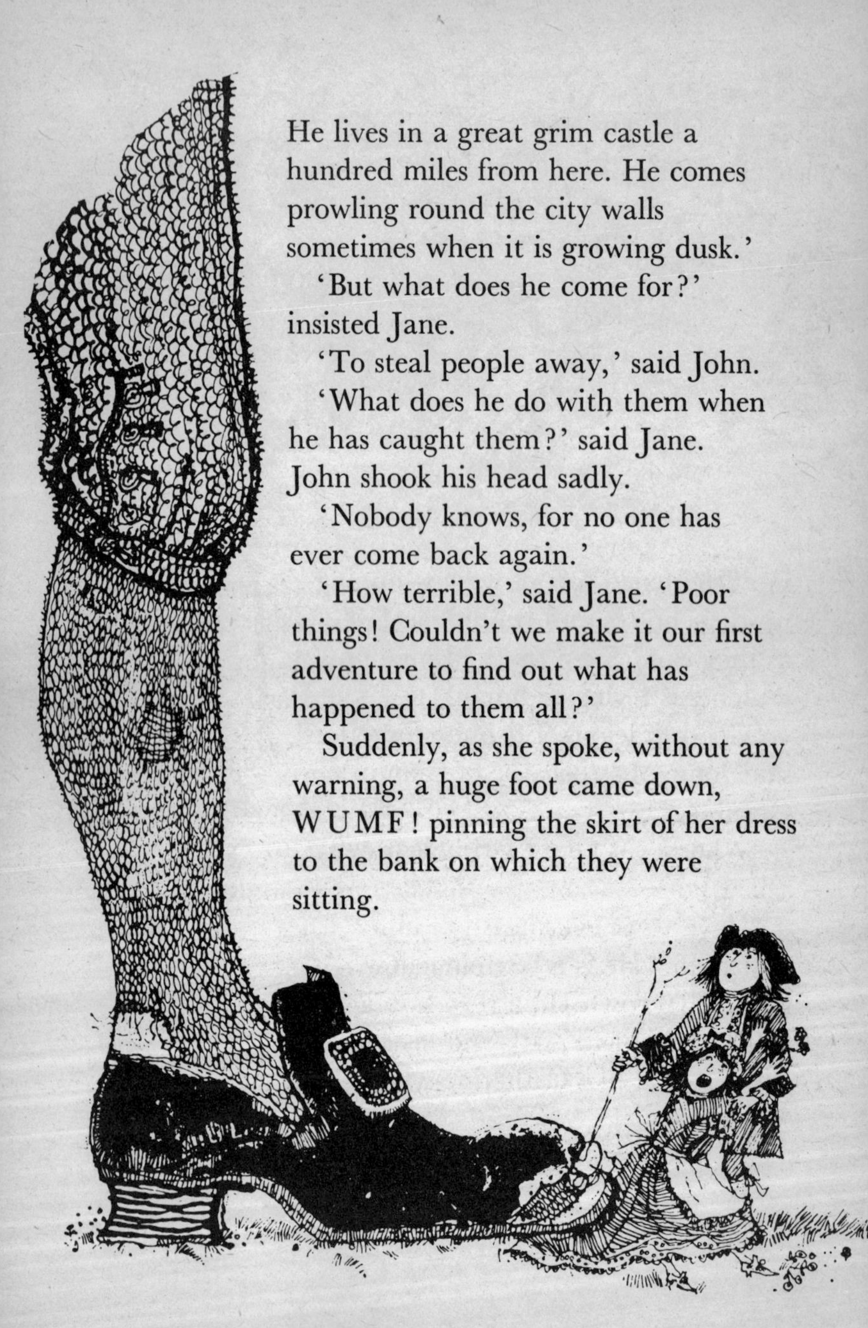

He lives in a great grim castle a hundred miles from here. He comes prowling round the city walls sometimes when it is growing dusk.'

'But what does he come for?' insisted Jane.

'To steal people away,' said John.

'What does he do with them when he has caught them?' said Jane. John shook his head sadly.

'Nobody knows, for no one has ever come back again.'

'How terrible,' said Jane. 'Poor things! Couldn't we make it our first adventure to find out what has happened to them all?'

Suddenly, as she spoke, without any warning, a huge foot came down, WUMF! pinning the skirt of her dress to the bank on which they were sitting.

'Help!' she cried in a frightened voice. 'It's the Giant!'

John snatched up a stick and prodded the great foot.

'Don't do that, it tickles!' rumbled Grimblegraw.

'Why don't you look where you're going?' John shouted up at him.

'Because my eyes whizz round like Catherine-wheels I can't see clearly down there. But why aren't you frightened of me like the other little mannikins? They generally squeal and try to run away. Of course I always catch them in the end, so they might as well not bother. Giving me all that extra trouble,' he grumbled.

As he stooped to peer at them, Grimblegraw grabbed Jane and John, and dropped them into his coat pocket, where they landed in a tangle of arms and legs.

'Well, this is an adventure, and no mistake!' said John, as they sorted themselves out in the darkness.

'These "mannikins" must be the poor people who are never seen again!'

'I don't like being stuffed in someone's dusty old pocket, with a grubby handkerchief,' said Jane.

'Nor do I,' said John, and he poked his head out and shouted, 'Hi! Grimblegraw! Can't you put us somewhere else? It's stuffy in here!'

The Giant began to laugh. John and Jane were nearly deafened by the noise.

'The cheek of you!' he said at last. 'But I like your spirit. All right, you can sit on my shoulders if you'd rather.'

Still laughing, Grimblegraw scooped them out of his pocket and sat them down, one on each side.

'You can hang on to my whiskers if you like,' he added.

As he spoke he turned and went striding away from the town. At first John and Jane, clinging to the jungle of the Giant's beard, were so interested

in the moving scene below them, as he strode over hills and valleys, forests and rivers, that they could think of nothing else.

'Where are you taking us?' asked Jane presently.

'Where I've taken all the others,' he answered; 'to my great grim castle.'

'But what for?' asked John.

'To cook and clean. With my whizzing eyes I can't see to do it for myself.'

'Why don't you go and capture someone your own size?' asked John indignantly.

'Because there is no one my size left,' said Grimblegraw sadly. 'When my ten tall brothers went off to see the world, they said I was no use after the Wuthering Witch made my eyes whizz round like Catherine-wheels.'

'But why did she do that? I mean, make your eyes whizz round?' asked Jane.

'Because I offended her,' replied Grimblegraw. 'It was quite by mistake.

There was I sitting in the sunshine, with my back against a mountain, and my hat over my nose, minding my own business. I was just dropping off to sleep when something went buzzing round my head. Well, I flapped my hand, as anybody would, and swatted it, thinking it was a bluebottle. But it wasn't a bluebottle. It was the Wuthering Witch, flying about on her broom-stick, and I'd knocked her clean off, so that she fell smack on her back on the ground.'

'Was she angry?' asked Jane.

'Angry?' said Grimblegraw. 'I picked her up with my finger and thumb, and sat her on my knee, and she hunched herself up, shaking with rage. When I said I was sorry, but I thought she was a bluebottle, it seemed to make it even worse. "Mistaken for a bluebottle! *Me*? The Wuthering Witch?" she screeched. "Don't you know that my magic is so powerful that if an ordinary human so much as looks at me I can turn him to stone! I shan't bother to do it to a great lumbering Giant like you: it would use up too much magic. But I shall get my own back for this. Little I may be to the likes of you, but I can make a big magic!"'

'And did she?' asked Jane. Grimblegraw nodded, so hard that Jane and John were nearly jolted off his shoulders.

'What did she do?' went on John, when they had wriggled themselves back to safety again.

'She pointed her two skinny forefingers at me, and muttered and mumbled some nonsense under her breath. When I clapped my hands to my face, for I felt something had happened to it, she cackled with laughter, and from that minute my eyes have whizzed round like Catherine-wheels. You can't imagine how awkward it is.'

'But haven't you asked her what to do to make yourself un-bewitched?' asked Jane.

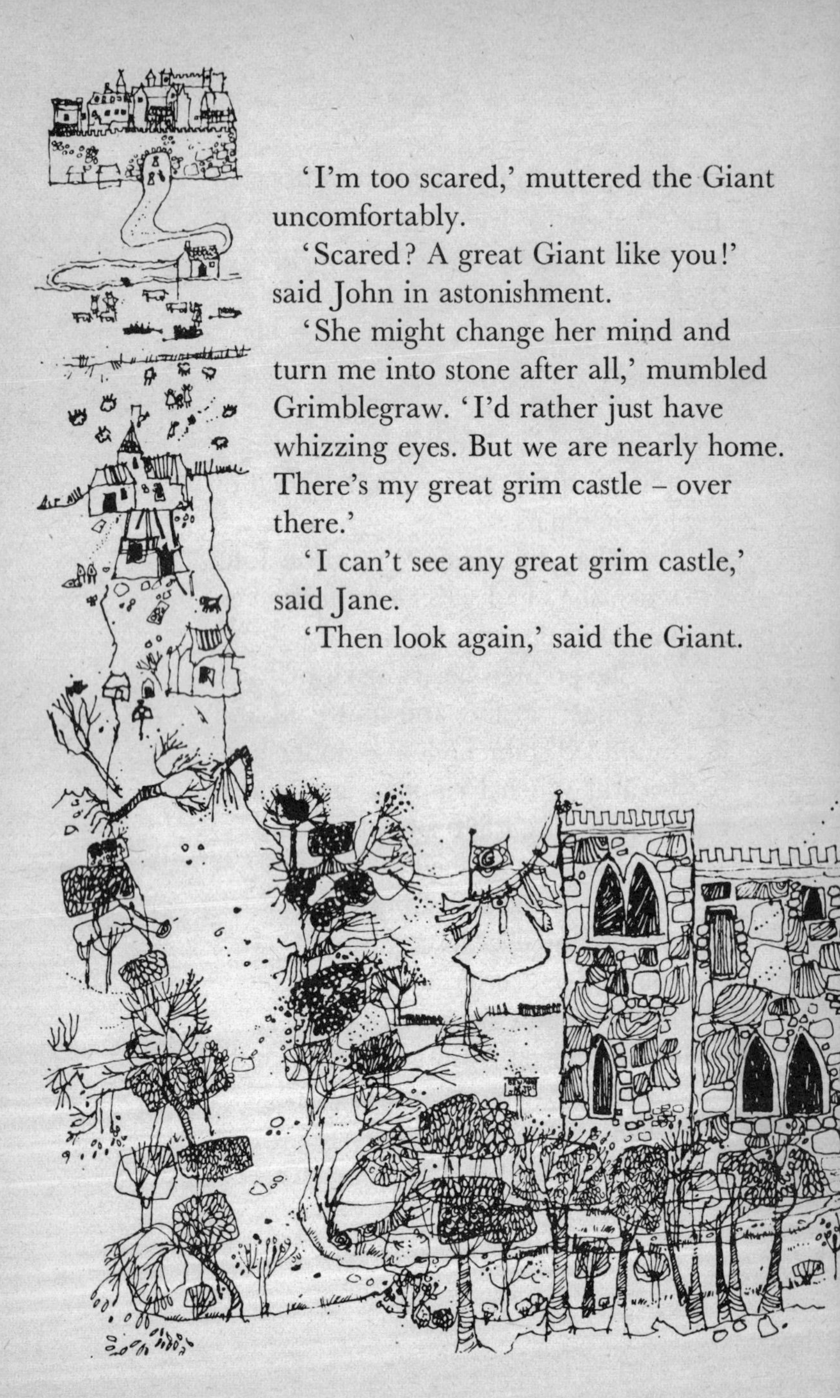

'I'm too scared,' muttered the Giant uncomfortably.

'Scared? A great Giant like you!' said John in astonishment.

'She might change her mind and turn me into stone after all,' mumbled Grimblegraw. 'I'd rather just have whizzing eyes. But we are nearly home. There's my great grim castle – over there.'

'I can't see any great grim castle,' said Jane.

'Then look again,' said the Giant.

Presently they realized that what at first they had thought was a towering great cliff in front of them was really the Giant's castle. Grimblegraw took a huge key from his other pocket, and unlocked an enormous door.

It clanged behind them, and after striding down endless passages, they came to the Giant's kitchen. Everything in it was giant-size: chairs, tables, pots and kettles.

'Where are the mannikins?' asked Jane. Grimblegraw nodded towards the shelves on which you would expect to see cups and saucers. Instead, there were rows and rows of unhappy-looking people sitting with dangling legs.

'That's where I puts 'em when I'm out, so that they can't get down and escape. Mannikins!' roared the Giant suddenly. 'Here are two more of you, to take the place of the ones who got in the way when I stamped yesterday. Show 'em how you go about your jobs. I'm hungry! I want my supper!'

He put John and Jane on the floor, and then he ſetched an enormous dustpan and brush, swept the mannikins from the shelves, and tipped them, helter skelter, on the ground.

Some of them ran to roll out enormous carrots and turnips, which were cut up by two men using a giant-sized knife like a two-handled saw. The small pieces they piled into the bowls of several tablespoons, arranged see-saw fashion over a row of egg-cups.

This done, some of the others jumped smartly on the handles of the spoons so that the vegetables flew up in a curve and fell – plop! – into a cauldron of water boiling on the fire.

Some of them lugged out a tablecloth as large as a tennis court, and others bowled plates and cups from the cupboard.

And every now and then Grimblegraw would jump up and roar, 'Faster! Faster! Or I shall stamp!'

And with a cry of fear the mannikins would scuttle round even more quickly.

'That always seems to get 'em going,' said the Giant. 'It's a funny thing,' he went on, 'but the ones who get in the way of my foot when I stamp aren't any use any more.

They don't seem to be the right shape somehow.'

'I'm not surprised!' said John.

'And then I have to go off to the town and hunt up some more mannikins to take their place,' he grumbled.

When the Giant had eaten supper, he sat back and went to sleep in his chair. At the first snore, the mannikins swarmed up the wrinkles of his stockings, and scrambled up on to the table any way they could, where they gobbled up every crumb they could find. John and Jane joined them.

'Caught you today, did he?' asked a young man who was sitting on the edge of a plate and licking his fingers. 'Poor things!'

'Is there no way we can escape?' asked Jane.

'We've tried many a time,' said the young man with a sigh. 'But every

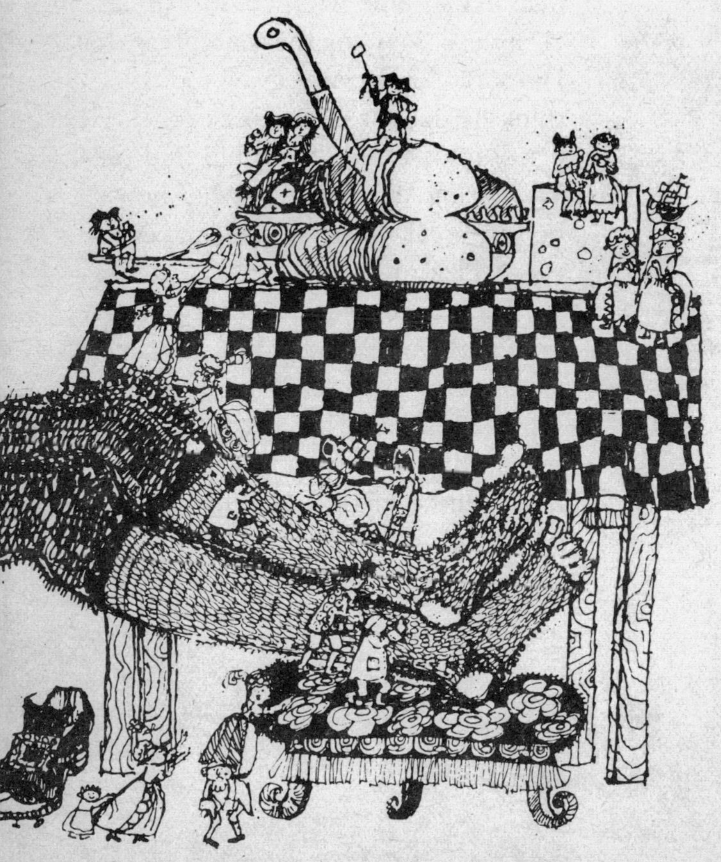

door and window is bolted and barred, and even if we could reach the locks they are too big and heavy for us to move.'

When they had been placed on the shelves for the night with the other mannikins, Jane whispered to John, 'I'm very sorry for the mannikins, but I'm sorry for Grimblegraw too. I think he doesn't mean to be cruel. He's just stupid. If only we could find the Wuthering Witch and ask her how he can break the spell that makes his eyes whizz round.'

'And get turned into stone ourselves? No thank you!' said John.

'But don't you see?' went on Jane. 'If his eyes could be cured, he would not need the mannikins any more, and then he might let them go.'

'All right,' said John, 'perhaps we could keep our eyes shut when we talk to the Wuthering Witch. Anything is better than just sitting on a shelf and dangling our legs. But first we've got to escape from the castle.' He nudged the old woman who was dozing beside him and asked: 'How does Grimblegraw know if any mannikins are missing, if his eyes are always whizzing round?'

'Every morning he weighs us on his great kitchen scales,' she said. 'If the weight is short he goes hunting for more people. Now leave me alone; I want to go to sleep.'

John lowered his voice and whispered to Jane, 'We must think as hard as we can. Between us we ought to be able to invent a plan of escape.' So they thought and thought.

Later that night John and Jane woke the other mannikins and explained the plan they had worked out, and what they wanted them to do.

In great excitement they all took off their belts and sashes and stockings. The women tore strips from their skirts and petticoats, and then they tied them all together into a long rope, and lowered John and Jane to the floor, who then climbed into the pocket of the sleeping giant and hauled the rope in after them.

'Good luck!' the mannikins whispered.

'Thunder and lightning!' roared Grimblegraw, when he weighed his prisoners next day. 'I'm two mannikins short again! I shall have to go out and hunt down a couple more!'

As he stumped off to the castle door, John and Jane tied the end of the rope to the button on his pocket flap,

and as he turned to lock the great door behind him, they let it down, and swarmed hand under hand down to the ground. Then they began to run.

They ran and ran until they reached a wide barren moor.

'Let's ask the old man standing over there if he can tell us the way to the Wuthering Witch,' said Jane. 'Why, it isn't a man: it's a statue!' she went on when they drew level with him.

'It isn't a statue,' said John, in an awed voice. 'It's a man who's been turned to stone, from his boots to his waistcoat buttons!'

'By the Wuthering Witch?' asked Jane.

John nodded. 'Let's ask at that cottage over there how we can find her.'

The woman who opened the door to to their knock welcomed them in.

'What are you doing here?' she said. Don't you know what danger you are in? You are only a stone's throw from the cave of the Wuthering Witch who will turn you to stone if you so much as look at her. Even my poor husband . . .' she broke off and wiped her eyes.

'We *must* find the Wuthering Witch,' said Jane, 'to ask her a question that only she can answer. Please tell us how to find her.'

'Then follow the Stone People, if you must go. They will lead you to her cave by the Magic Lake. But remember, whatever you do, do not look at her.'

'We will be very careful,' said Jane.

'Will she be in her cave if we go to find her now?' went on John.

'Not in her witch's shape she won't,' said the woman. 'All night long she disguises herself as a Snarling Beast while she goes about her wicked doings; but towards dawn the Beast slinks back to the cave, they say, to drink a magic potion. Then it goes down to the lake. Only by bathing in it can she be born again as a witch for the daylight hours. She sinks to the bottom of the lake, I've been told, and presently there is a great swirling of waves and she rises from the water as a little child and hurries back to the cave. But in that short distance she grows up, as she runs, until just before she disappears inside she becomes an old wicked, white-haired witch again.'

'But how can we ask her a question while all this is happening?' asked Jane.

'Just before she disappears into the cave as her old self, and then only, you can ask your question, and she is bound to answer.

'That is what all the Stone People came to do, but they couldn't resist the temptation to look at her, and so they were turned into stony statues.

Take my advice, my dears, and go home before it is too late.'

John and Jane shook their heads, then they thanked the woman and although night had fallen, they set out once more. The moonlight shone on more Stone People, men, women, and even children.

Just as day was breaking, they came upon the dark mouth of the cave, and the glimmering waters of the lake. Safely hidden among some bushes, they waited for the dawn.

As the sun began to rise, from the depths of the cave they heard a snarling, yarling sound. They shrank back into the bushes, not daring to look, but the snarling sound passed

them, and grew fainter, as the Beast went down to the lake to bathe.

When it had passed them Jane peered through her fingers at the ground.

'Look at the paw marks it has left in the sand!' she said.

'Let's follow them down the slope to the lake,' said John. 'Then we can see where she is going without looking at her.'

Shielding their eyes with their hands they followed the paw marks down to the water's edge, where the little lapping waves swallowed them up. They waited breathlessly for what seemed an age. 'Suppose she comes out of the lake in quite a different place?' said Jane. 'Then we might lose her altogether, and miss the right moment to ask our question.'

Just as she spoke there was a great swirling of water.

'She's coming out!' shouted John. 'Shut your eyes and count ten, then we can look for her footprints again. One, two, three . . .' Together they counted ten, then they opened their eyes.

'Look over there!' cried Jane.

John looked where she was pointing.

'The footprints of a tiny child!' he whispered.

'Leading away from the water and back to the cave!' went on Jane.

'And getting bigger as they go!' said John.

Breathless with excitement they watched the footprints grow larger and larger as they went up the beach towards the cave, and as they went a withering, wuthering voice began to whisper, 'Look at me! Look at me!'

As the footprints grew bigger, so the voice grew louder, until just before they reached the cave the marks in the sand became those of a gnarled-footed old woman, and the crooning became a sharp command.

'Look at ME! LOOK – AT – ME!'

'We won't look!' cried John, squeezing his eyes tight shut.

'We want to ask you a question!' said Jane.

'Then ask, and I am bound to answer!' said the Witch in a harsh, monotonous voice.

'Wuthering Witch!' called John, with his head still bent. 'How can we cure the whizzing eyes of Giant Grimblegraw?'

'You have but to touch his eyelids with water from the Magic Lake,' she replied, in the same monotonous voice.

'Is that all?' cried Jane, starting up and clapping her hands. 'Oh, thank you – thank . . . ' her voice tailed off.

'Don't look up!' shouted John. But he was too late. Jane was already turned to stone. And the Witch had disappeared into the cave.

'Jane, Jane!' he cried. But of course she could not answer. He turned and shouted, 'Wicked, wicked Wuthering Witch! I don't care what happens to

Grimblegraw and the mannikins if only you will make Jane alive again!' But the only answer was a low cackling laugh from the depths of the cave.

He turned to the statue which had once been Jane: 'Don't despair,' he cried. 'First, I shall take the magic water to Giant Grimblegraw. Then I will come back, and, somehow, I shall rescue you!'

He ran down to the lake, and filled one of his shoes with the precious water. 'Poor, poor Jane! Before I go, I'll just say good-bye,' he thought.

But just as he reached her, he stumbled and fell, and the magic water splashed all over her cold, grey feet. As he got up again, he suddenly saw they were no longer made of stone, and from her ankles upwards slowly rose a tide of colour, until at last her rosy cheeks bunched into a wide smile. The spell was broken.

'Oh John!' she cried. 'However did you do it?'

'It must have been the water from the lake,' said John. 'I spilt it over your feet when I fell over. Before we go let's sprinkle it on all the Stone People we can find!'

'But – the Wuthering Witch . . . ?' began Jane.

'I don't think we need worry about her for a little,' said John. 'Listen!' From inside the cave came the unmistakable sound of snoring.

'Come on, before she wakes!'

They raced down to the lake and each with a shoeful of water hurried from one statue to another. Splashed with the smallest drop, each one came to life, till there was not a stone figure left.

Then John and Jane said good-bye, and amid the cheers of the rescued people they set off across the moor, slowly and carefully, so that not a drop of the precious water should be spilt from the shoe.

When they reached the castle, Grimblegraw was just returning from his day's hunting. As he unlocked the great door, they slipped in at his heels.

As soon as he entered the kitchen, he roared, 'I've had no luck today, I've caught no mannikins, so you'll have to work that much harder to make up for it. Hurry, or I shall stamp!' And he lifted a great foot.

'Stop! Stop!' shouted John and Jane. 'We have just come back from the Wuthering Witch, and she has told us how to cure your poor whizzing eyes!'

'Sit down on the floor,' said John, 'and close your eyes.' There was a scuttling of mannikins to safety as he obeyed.

Then, very carefully, lest the precious water should spill, they climbed up the Giant, passing the shoe from one to the other at the steepest places, using creases and buttonholes as footholds. Up they went, till at last they stood on the tangle of his bristling beard.

Then, standing on tiptoe, they touched each of his huge eyelids with a finger dipped in the magic water. This done they scrambled down again.

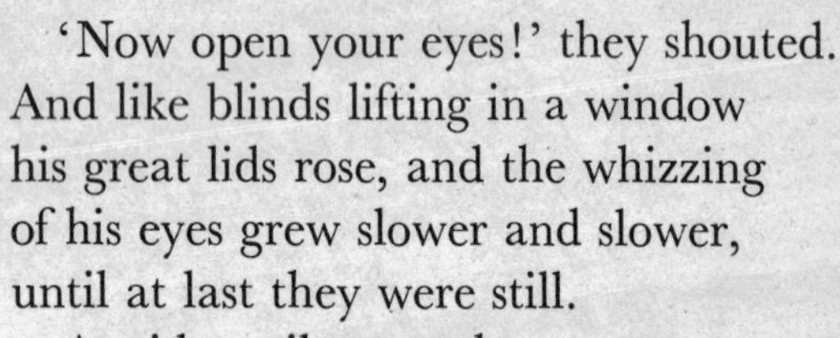

'Now open your eyes!' they shouted. And like blinds lifting in a window his great lids rose, and the whizzing of his eyes grew slower and slower, until at last they were still.

A wide smile spread across Grimblegraw's face, and a cheer went up from the watching mannikins.

'I can see once more! Oh joy! Oh

joy!' he cried. 'Tomorrow, I shall join my ten tall brothers. I need you no longer, my little mannikins.' And he opened the great door to the outside world.

Singing and laughing, they trooped out, and away to their homes. But when the Giant returned to the kitchen, to his surprise he found John and Jane still there.

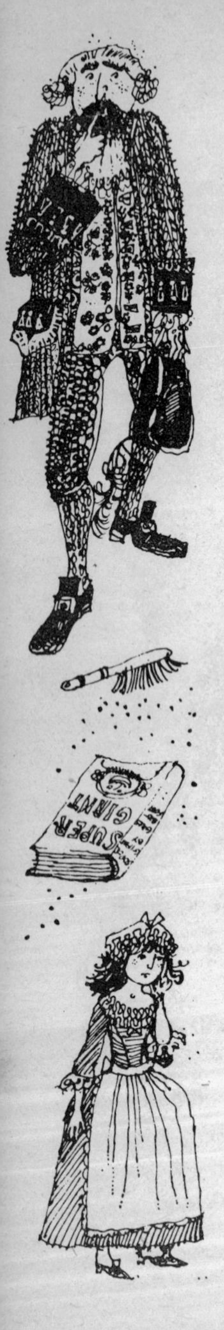

'What now, little people?' he said. 'Don't you want to go home too?'

'The trouble is this,' said John with a frown. 'If I go back, I shall have to marry that tiresome Princess Yolanda. And the only girl I want to marry is Jane.'

A slow smile spread over Jane's face. 'And the only person I want to marry is John. I suppose, by any chance, your name isn't really – Benedict?'

'However did you guess?' he answered in astonishment.

'Because my name is Yolanda! And all this time we thought we were running away from one another!'

And they began to laugh. When they explained the joke, Grimblegraw laughed with them, and they laughed and laughed till their sides ached.

Then the grateful Giant carried them back to the town, and of course they were married. The people sang

and danced in the streets and the bells rang until the slates flew off the steeples. Everyone rejoiced.

But the ones who rejoiced most of all were Prince Benedict and Princess Yolanda.

About the Author

Barbara Sleigh was born in 1906 in Warwickshire. Her father was an artist and as a small child she spent a great deal of time messing about in his studio. While he worked he told her endless stories.

Educated at St Catherine's School, Bramley, she later went to an art school, then took an art teacher's training and taught both boys and girls in the Black Country. At about this time she wrote stories for children for the new-fangled radio.

In the 1930s she became a lecturer at Goldsmith's College, joined the staff of the BBC Children's Hour, and married David Davis, who who was later to become head of Children's Hour.

As well as writing plays and stories for radio, Miss Sleigh began writing for publishing with *Carbonel* in 1955 and that book, as well as *Carbonel and Calidor* and *The Kingdom of Carbonel*, has been published in Puffins, and *Ninety-Nine Dragons* in Young Puffins.

Her hobbies are cats, the theatre and picture galleries.

Also by Barbara Sleigh

Ninety-Nine Dragons

'I think sheep are soppy,' said Ben scornfully, so instead he sent dragons over a gate to help him to go to sleep. But he hadn't intended the ninety-nine greedy dragons to land in the same field as his sister's fifty woolly sheep!

Some Other Young Puffins

Saturday By Seven
Penelope Farmer

Peter should have been saving for a month to get the money needed to go to camp with the Cubs. Now there is only one day left, and how can he possibly earn it in time?

The Worst Witch
Jill Murphy

Mildred Hubble had a reputation for being the worst pupil in Miss Cackle's school for witches. So when things started to go wrong at the Hallowe'en celebrations, she was naturally at the centre of it all.

Carrot Tops
Joan Wyatt

Fifteen stories of everyday events like making a jelly, growing a carrot-top garden, visiting Granny – all tinged with the make-believe that young children love.

Where Matthew Lives
Teresa Verschoyle

Happy stories about a little boy exploring his new home, a cottage tucked away by the sea.

Adventures of Sam Pig
Alison Uttley

Ten funny and magical stories about Alison Uttley's best-loved creation. For children of five to nine.

Satchkin Patchkin

Helen Morgan

Satchkin Patchkin, a little green magic man, lives in an apple tree like a leaf. These stories about him make a book that 'reads aloud so well it is almost a waste to sit alone and read it' – *The Times Literary Supplement*

Stories for Under-Fives
Stories for Five-Year-Olds
Stories for Six-Year-Olds
Stories for Seven-Year-Olds
Stories for Eight-Year-Olds

Sara and Stephen Corrin

Celebrated anthologies of stories especially chosen for each age group and tested in the classroom by the editors.

The Little Sparrow *and* Midnight Patrol

Frances Eagar

Two delightful stories about Laura and her brother Harry, in which they befriend a baby sparrow that has fallen out of its nest, and spend a night camping in their wild garden, on jungle patrol.

Joseph's Bear

Evelyn Davies

The bear was the best thing that Joseph had ever owned, but when you love something you may have to make a hard decision.

The Village Dinosaur

Phyllis Arkle

The cranes had lifted something extraordinary out of the quarry – a real dinosaur, and it seemed to be waking up! Jed Watkins was the first to recognize it, and wanted to keep it in the village as a pet, but the stuffy Parish Clerk wanted to get rid of it before it did any damage.

My Dog Sunday

Leila Berg

Ben longs for a dog of his own, but no one will let him have one. Then one magical Sunday he meets a huge, friendly, shaggy dog in the Park, and nobody seems to own him . . .

Albert's Circus

Alison Jezard

Albert the bear and his friends think they are off for a quiet holiday in the country – but in no time at all they are hard at work putting on their very own circus show, and what fun it all is!

The Little Girl and the Tiny Doll

Edward and Aingelda Ardizzone

A tiny doll is dropped into a grocery store's deep-freeze and endures the arctic conditions with the help of a little girl.